PERSONAL

GOLF SCORE TRACKER

THIS BELONGS TO

PHONE NUMBER

SCORE CARD

LOCATION				COURSE			
PAR		DATE		START TIME		FINISH TIME	
WEATHER & WIND				OTHER PLAYERS			
TEE COLOR				HANDICAP		HOLES PLAYED	

FRONT NINE									
HOLE	PAR	DISTANCE	STROKE INDEX	FAIRWAY	HAZARD	PUTTS	SCORE	+ / -	
1									
2									
3									
4									
5									
6									
7									
8									
9									
TOTAL									

BACK NINE									
HOLE	PAR	DISTANCE	STROKE INDEX	FAIRWAY	HAZARD	PUTTS	SCORE	+ / -	
10									
11									
12									
13									
14									
15									
16									
17									
18									
TOTAL									

GAME RECAP			
FRONT 9 STROKES		BACK 9 STROKES	
FRONT 9 ADJUSTED SCORE		BACK 9 ADJUSTED SCORE	
TOTAL STROKES		TOTAL ADJUSTED SCORE	

STROKE RECAP			
EAGLES		BIRDIES	
PARS		BOGEYS	
DOUBLE BOGEYS		OTHER	
PENALTY STROKES		PUTTS	
FAIRWAY SHOTS			

NOTES / AREAS FOR IMPROVEMENT

. . . .

. . . .

. . . .

. . . .

. . . .

. . . .

. . . .

. . . .

. . . .

. . . .

. . . .

. . . .

SCORE CARD

LOCATION				COURSE				
PAR		DATE		START TIME		FINISH TIME		
WEATHER & WIND				OTHER PLAYERS				
TEE COLOR				HANDICAP		HOLES PLAYED		

FRONT NINE								
HOLE	PAR	DISTANCE	STROKE INDEX	FAIRWAY	HAZARD	PUTTS	SCORE	+ / -
1								
2								
3								
4								
5								
6								
7								
8								
9								
TOTAL								

BACK NINE								
HOLE	PAR	DISTANCE	STROKE INDEX	FAIRWAY	HAZARD	PUTTS	SCORE	+ / -
10								
11								
12								
13								
14								
15								
16								
17								
18								
TOTAL								

GAME RECAP			
FRONT 9 STROKES		BACK 9 STROKES	
FRONT 9 ADJUSTED SCORE		BACK 9 ADJUSTED SCORE	
TOTAL STROKES		TOTAL ADJUSTED SCORE	

STROKE RECAP			
EAGLES		BIRDIES	
PARS		BOGEYS	
DOUBLE BOGEYS		OTHER	
PENALTY STROKES		PUTTS	
FAIRWAY SHOTS			

NOTES / AREAS FOR IMPROVEMENT

SCORE CARD

LOCATION				COURSE					
PAR		DATE		START TIME			FINISH TIME		
WEATHER & WIND				OTHER PLAYERS					
TEE COLOR				HANDICAP			HOLES PLAYED		

FRONT NINE									
HOLE	PAR	DISTANCE	STROKE INDEX	FAIRWAY	HAZARD	PUTTS	SCORE	+ / -	
1									
2									
3									
4									
5									
6									
7									
8									
9									
TOTAL									

BACK NINE									
HOLE	PAR	DISTANCE	STROKE INDEX	FAIRWAY	HAZARD	PUTTS	SCORE	+ / -	
10									
11									
12									
13									
14									
15									
16									
17									
18									
TOTAL									

GAME RECAP			
FRONT 9 STROKES		BACK 9 STROKES	
FRONT 9 ADJUSTED SCORE		BACK 9 ADJUSTED SCORE	
TOTAL STROKES		TOTAL ADJUSTED SCORE	

STROKE RECAP			
EAGLES		BIRDIES	
PARS		BOGEYS	
DOUBLE BOGEYS		OTHER	
PENALTY STROKES		PUTTS	
FAIRWAY SHOTS			

NOTES / AREAS FOR IMPROVEMENT

....

....

....

....

....

....

....

....

....

....

....

....

SCORE CARD

LOCATION				COURSE				
PAR		DATE		START TIME		FINISH TIME		
WEATHER & WIND				OTHER PLAYERS				
TEE COLOR				HANDICAP		HOLES PLAYED		

FRONT NINE									
HOLE	PAR	DISTANCE	STROKE INDEX	FAIRWAY	HAZARD	PUTTS	SCORE	+ / -	
1									
2									
3									
4									
5									
6									
7									
8									
9									
TOTAL									

BACK NINE									
HOLE	PAR	DISTANCE	STROKE INDEX	FAIRWAY	HAZARD	PUTTS	SCORE	+ / -	
10									
11									
12									
13									
14									
15									
16									
17									
18									
TOTAL									

GAME RECAP			
FRONT 9 STROKES		BACK 9 STROKES	
FRONT 9 ADJUSTED SCORE		BACK 9 ADJUSTED SCORE	
TOTAL STROKES		TOTAL ADJUSTED SCORE	

STROKE RECAP			
EAGLES		BIRDIES	
PARS		BOGEYS	
DOUBLE BOGEYS		OTHER	
PENALTY STROKES		PUTTS	
FAIRWAY SHOTS			

NOTES / AREAS FOR IMPROVEMENT

....

....

....

....

....

....

....

....

....

....

....

....

SCORE CARD

LOCATION		COURSE		
PAR	DATE	START TIME	FINISH TIME	
WEATHER & WIND		OTHER PLAYERS		
TEE COLOR		HANDICAP	HOLES PLAYED	

FRONT NINE									
HOLE	PAR	DISTANCE	STROKE INDEX	FAIRWAY	HAZARD	PUTTS	SCORE	+ / -	
1									
2									
3									
4									
5									
6									
7									
8									
9									
TOTAL									

BACK NINE									
HOLE	PAR	DISTANCE	STROKE INDEX	FAIRWAY	HAZARD	PUTTS	SCORE	+ / -	
10									
11									
12									
13									
14									
15									
16									
17									
18									
TOTAL									

GAME RECAP			
FRONT 9 STROKES		BACK 9 STROKES	
FRONT 9 ADJUSTED SCORE		BACK 9 ADJUSTED SCORE	
TOTAL STROKES		TOTAL ADJUSTED SCORE	

STROKE RECAP			
EAGLES		BIRDIES	
PARS		BOGEYS	
DOUBLE BOGEYS		OTHER	
PENALTY STROKES		PUTTS	
FAIRWAY SHOTS			

NOTES / AREAS FOR IMPROVEMENT

SCORE CARD

LOCATION			COURSE			
PAR		DATE		START TIME		FINISH TIME
WEATHER & WIND			OTHER PLAYERS			
TEE COLOR			HANDICAP		HOLES PLAYED	

FRONT NINE

HOLE	PAR	DISTANCE	STROKE INDEX	FAIRWAY	HAZARD	PUTTS	SCORE	+ / -	
1									
2									
3									
4									
5									
6									
7									
8									
9									
TOTAL									

BACK NINE

HOLE	PAR	DISTANCE	STROKE INDEX	FAIRWAY	HAZARD	PUTTS	SCORE	+ / -	
10									
11									
12									
13									
14									
15									
16									
17									
18									
TOTAL									

GAME RECAP			
FRONT 9 STROKES		BACK 9 STROKES	
FRONT 9 ADJUSTED SCORE		BACK 9 ADJUSTED SCORE	
TOTAL STROKES		TOTAL ADJUSTED SCORE	

STROKE RECAP			
EAGLES		BIRDIES	
PARS		BOGEYS	
DOUBLE BOGEYS		OTHER	
PENALTY STROKES		PUTTS	
FAIRWAY SHOTS			

NOTES / AREAS FOR IMPROVEMENT

....

....

....

....

....

....

....

....

....

....

....

....

....

SCORE CARD

LOCATION			COURSE			
PAR		DATE		START TIME		FINISH TIME
WEATHER & WIND			OTHER PLAYERS			
TEE COLOR			HANDICAP		HOLES PLAYED	

FRONT NINE									
HOLE	PAR	DISTANCE	STROKE INDEX	FAIRWAY	HAZARD	PUTTS	SCORE	+ / -	
1									
2									
3									
4									
5									
6									
7									
8									
9									
TOTAL									

BACK NINE									
HOLE	PAR	DISTANCE	STROKE INDEX	FAIRWAY	HAZARD	PUTTS	SCORE	+ / -	
10									
11									
12									
13									
14									
15									
16									
17									
18									
TOTAL									

GAME RECAP			
FRONT 9 STROKES		BACK 9 STROKES	
FRONT 9 ADJUSTED SCORE		BACK 9 ADJUSTED SCORE	
TOTAL STROKES		TOTAL ADJUSTED SCORE	

STROKE RECAP			
EAGLES		BIRDIES	
PARS		BOGEYS	
DOUBLE BOGEYS		OTHER	
PENALTY STROKES		PUTTS	
FAIRWAY SHOTS			

NOTES / AREAS FOR IMPROVEMENT

....

....

....

....

....

....

....

....

....

....

....

....

....

SCORE CARD

LOCATION				COURSE			
PAR		DATE		START TIME		FINISH TIME	
WEATHER & WIND				OTHER PLAYERS			
TEE COLOR				HANDICAP		HOLES PLAYED	

FRONT NINE

HOLE	PAR	DISTANCE	STROKE INDEX	FAIRWAY	HAZARD	PUTTS	SCORE	+/-	
1									
2									
3									
4									
5									
6									
7									
8									
9									
TOTAL									

BACK NINE

HOLE	PAR	DISTANCE	STROKE INDEX	FAIRWAY	HAZARD	PUTTS	SCORE	+/-	
10									
11									
12									
13									
14									
15									
16									
17									
18									
TOTAL									

GAME RECAP			
FRONT 9 STROKES		BACK 9 STROKES	
FRONT 9 ADJUSTED SCORE		BACK 9 ADJUSTED SCORE	
TOTAL STROKES		TOTAL ADJUSTED SCORE	

STROKE RECAP			
EAGLES		BIRDIES	
PARS		BOGEYS	
DOUBLE BOGEYS		OTHER	
PENALTY STROKES		PUTTS	
FAIRWAY SHOTS			

NOTES / AREAS FOR IMPROVEMENT

SCORE CARD

LOCATION		COURSE			
PAR	DATE	START TIME		FINISH TIME	
WEATHER & WIND		OTHER PLAYERS			
TEE COLOR		HANDICAP		HOLES PLAYED	

FRONT NINE								
HOLE	PAR	DISTANCE	STROKE INDEX	FAIRWAY	HAZARD	PUTTS	SCORE	+ / -
1								
2								
3								
4								
5								
6								
7								
8								
9								
TOTAL								

BACK NINE								
HOLE	PAR	DISTANCE	STROKE INDEX	FAIRWAY	HAZARD	PUTTS	SCORE	+ / -
10								
11								
12								
13								
14								
15								
16								
17								
18								
TOTAL								

GAME RECAP			
FRONT 9 STROKES		BACK 9 STROKES	
FRONT 9 ADJUSTED SCORE		BACK 9 ADJUSTED SCORE	
TOTAL STROKES		TOTAL ADJUSTED SCORE	

STROKE RECAP			
EAGLES		BIRDIES	
PARS		BOGEYS	
DOUBLE BOGEYS		OTHER	
PENALTY STROKES		PUTTS	
FAIRWAY SHOTS			

NOTES / AREAS FOR IMPROVEMENT

SCORE CARD

LOCATION				COURSE				
PAR		DATE		START TIME		FINISH TIME		
WEATHER & WIND				OTHER PLAYERS				
TEE COLOR				HANDICAP		HOLES PLAYED		

FRONT NINE								
HOLE	PAR	DISTANCE	STROKE INDEX	FAIRWAY	HAZARD	PUTTS	SCORE	+ / -
1								
2								
3								
4								
5								
6								
7								
8								
9								
TOTAL								

BACK NINE								
HOLE	PAR	DISTANCE	STROKE INDEX	FAIRWAY	HAZARD	PUTTS	SCORE	+ / -
10								
11								
12								
13								
14								
15								
16								
17								
18								
TOTAL								

GAME RECAP			
FRONT 9 STROKES		BACK 9 STROKES	
FRONT 9 ADJUSTED SCORE		BACK 9 ADJUSTED SCORE	
TOTAL STROKES		TOTAL ADJUSTED SCORE	

STROKE RECAP			
EAGLES		BIRDIES	
PARS		BOGEYS	
DOUBLE BOGEYS		OTHER	
PENALTY STROKES		PUTTS	
FAIRWAY SHOTS			

NOTES / AREAS FOR IMPROVEMENT

....

....

....

....

....

....

....

....

....

....

....

....

....

SCORE CARD

LOCATION			COURSE		
PAR	DATE		START TIME	FINISH TIME	
WEATHER & WIND			OTHER PLAYERS		
TEE COLOR			HANDICAP	HOLES PLAYED	

FRONT NINE

HOLE	PAR	DISTANCE	STROKE INDEX	FAIRWAY	HAZARD	PUTTS	SCORE	+ / -	
1									
2									
3									
4									
5									
6									
7									
8									
9									
TOTAL									

BACK NINE

HOLE	PAR	DISTANCE	STROKE INDEX	FAIRWAY	HAZARD	PUTTS	SCORE	+ / -	
10									
11									
12									
13									
14									
15									
16									
17									
18									
TOTAL									

GAME RECAP			
FRONT 9 STROKES		BACK 9 STROKES	
FRONT 9 ADJUSTED SCORE		BACK 9 ADJUSTED SCORE	
TOTAL STROKES		TOTAL ADJUSTED SCORE	

STROKE RECAP			
EAGLES		BIRDIES	
PARS		BOGEYS	
DOUBLE BOGEYS		OTHER	
PENALTY STROKES		PUTTS	
FAIRWAY SHOTS			

NOTES / AREAS FOR IMPROVEMENT

SCORE CARD

LOCATION		COURSE			
PAR	DATE	START TIME		FINISH TIME	
WEATHER & WIND		OTHER PLAYERS			
TEE COLOR		HANDICAP		HOLES PLAYED	

FRONT NINE								
HOLE	PAR	DISTANCE	STROKE INDEX	FAIRWAY	HAZARD	PUTTS	SCORE	+ / -
1								
2								
3								
4								
5								
6								
7								
8								
9								
TOTAL								

BACK NINE								
HOLE	PAR	DISTANCE	STROKE INDEX	FAIRWAY	HAZARD	PUTTS	SCORE	+ / -
10								
11								
12								
13								
14								
15								
16								
17								
18								
TOTAL								

GAME RECAP			
FRONT 9 STROKES		BACK 9 STROKES	
FRONT 9 ADJUSTED SCORE		BACK 9 ADJUSTED SCORE	
TOTAL STROKES		TOTAL ADJUSTED SCORE	

STROKE RECAP			
EAGLES		BIRDIES	
PARS		BOGEYS	
DOUBLE BOGEYS		OTHER	
PENALTY STROKES		PUTTS	
FAIRWAY SHOTS			

NOTES / AREAS FOR IMPROVEMENT

....

....

....

....

....

....

....

....

....

....

....

....

SCORE CARD

LOCATION			COURSE			
PAR		DATE		START TIME		FINISH TIME
WEATHER & WIND			OTHER PLAYERS			
TEE COLOR			HANDICAP		HOLES PLAYED	

FRONT NINE

HOLE	PAR	DISTANCE	STROKE INDEX	FAIRWAY	HAZARD	PUTTS	SCORE	+ / -	
1									
2									
3									
4									
5									
6									
7									
8									
9									
TOTAL									

BACK NINE

HOLE	PAR	DISTANCE	STROKE INDEX	FAIRWAY	HAZARD	PUTTS	SCORE	+ / -	
10									
11									
12									
13									
14									
15									
16									
17									
18									
TOTAL									

GAME RECAP			
FRONT 9 STROKES		BACK 9 STROKES	
FRONT 9 ADJUSTED SCORE		BACK 9 ADJUSTED SCORE	
TOTAL STROKES		TOTAL ADJUSTED SCORE	

STROKE RECAP			
EAGLES		BIRDIES	
PARS		BOGEYS	
DOUBLE BOGEYS		OTHER	
PENALTY STROKES		PUTTS	
FAIRWAY SHOTS			

NOTES / AREAS FOR IMPROVEMENT

SCORE CARD

LOCATION				COURSE			
PAR		DATE		START TIME		FINISH TIME	
WEATHER & WIND				OTHER PLAYERS			
TEE COLOR				HANDICAP		HOLES PLAYED	

FRONT NINE									
HOLE	PAR	DISTANCE	STROKE INDEX	FAIRWAY	HAZARD	PUTTS	SCORE	+ / -	
1									
2									
3									
4									
5									
6									
7									
8									
9									
TOTAL									

BACK NINE									
HOLE	PAR	DISTANCE	STROKE INDEX	FAIRWAY	HAZARD	PUTTS	SCORE	+ / -	
10									
11									
12									
13									
14									
15									
16									
17									
18									
TOTAL									

GAME RECAP			
FRONT 9 STROKES		BACK 9 STROKES	
FRONT 9 ADJUSTED SCORE		BACK 9 ADJUSTED SCORE	
TOTAL STROKES		TOTAL ADJUSTED SCORE	

STROKE RECAP			
EAGLES		BIRDIES	
PARS		BOGEYS	
DOUBLE BOGEYS		OTHER	
PENALTY STROKES		PUTTS	
FAIRWAY SHOTS			

NOTES / AREAS FOR IMPROVEMENT

....

....

....

....

....

....

....

....

....

....

....

....

SCORE CARD

LOCATION				COURSE				
PAR		DATE		START TIME		FINISH TIME		
WEATHER & WIND				OTHER PLAYERS				
TEE COLOR				HANDICAP		HOLES PLAYED		

FRONT NINE									
HOLE	PAR	DISTANCE	STROKE INDEX	FAIRWAY	HAZARD	PUTTS	SCORE	+ / -	
1									
2									
3									
4									
5									
6									
7									
8									
9									
TOTAL									

BACK NINE									
HOLE	PAR	DISTANCE	STROKE INDEX	FAIRWAY	HAZARD	PUTTS	SCORE	+ / -	
10									
11									
12									
13									
14									
15									
16									
17									
18									
TOTAL									

GAME RECAP			
FRONT 9 STROKES		BACK 9 STROKES	
FRONT 9 ADJUSTED SCORE		BACK 9 ADJUSTED SCORE	
TOTAL STROKES		TOTAL ADJUSTED SCORE	

STROKE RECAP			
EAGLES		BIRDIES	
PARS		BOGEYS	
DOUBLE BOGEYS		OTHER	
PENALTY STROKES		PUTTS	
FAIRWAY SHOTS			

NOTES / AREAS FOR IMPROVEMENT

....

....

....

....

....

....

....

....

....

....

....

SCORE CARD

LOCATION				COURSE				
PAR		DATE		START TIME		FINISH TIME		
WEATHER & WIND				OTHER PLAYERS				
TEE COLOR				HANDICAP		HOLES PLAYED		

FRONT NINE									
HOLE	PAR	DISTANCE	STROKE INDEX	FAIRWAY	HAZARD	PUTTS	SCORE	+ / -	
1									
2									
3									
4									
5									
6									
7									
8									
9									
TOTAL									

BACK NINE									
HOLE	PAR	DISTANCE	STROKE INDEX	FAIRWAY	HAZARD	PUTTS	SCORE	+ / -	
10									
11									
12									
13									
14									
15									
16									
17									
18									
TOTAL									

GAME RECAP			
FRONT 9 STROKES		BACK 9 STROKES	
FRONT 9 ADJUSTED SCORE		BACK 9 ADJUSTED SCORE	
TOTAL STROKES		TOTAL ADJUSTED SCORE	

STROKE RECAP			
EAGLES		BIRDIES	
PARS		BOGEYS	
DOUBLE BOGEYS		OTHER	
PENALTY STROKES		PUTTS	
FAIRWAY SHOTS			

NOTES / AREAS FOR IMPROVEMENT

SCORE CARD

LOCATION				COURSE				
PAR		DATE		START TIME		FINISH TIME		
WEATHER & WIND				OTHER PLAYERS				
TEE COLOR				HANDICAP		HOLES PLAYED		

FRONT NINE									
HOLE	PAR	DISTANCE	STROKE INDEX	FAIRWAY	HAZARD	PUTTS	SCORE	+ / -	
1									
2									
3									
4									
5									
6									
7									
8									
9									
TOTAL									

BACK NINE									
HOLE	PAR	DISTANCE	STROKE INDEX	FAIRWAY	HAZARD	PUTTS	SCORE	+ / -	
10									
11									
12									
13									
14									
15									
16									
17									
18									
TOTAL									

GAME RECAP			
FRONT 9 STROKES		BACK 9 STROKES	
FRONT 9 ADJUSTED SCORE		BACK 9 ADJUSTED SCORE	
TOTAL STROKES		TOTAL ADJUSTED SCORE	

STROKE RECAP			
EAGLES		BIRDIES	
PARS		BOGEYS	
DOUBLE BOGEYS		OTHER	
PENALTY STROKES		PUTTS	
FAIRWAY SHOTS			

NOTES / AREAS FOR IMPROVEMENT

SCORE CARD

LOCATION				COURSE				
PAR		DATE		START TIME		FINISH TIME		
WEATHER & WIND				OTHER PLAYERS				
TEE COLOR				HANDICAP		HOLES PLAYED		

FRONT NINE

HOLE	PAR	DISTANCE	STROKE INDEX	FAIRWAY	HAZARD	PUTTS	SCORE	+ / -	
1									
2									
3									
4									
5									
6									
7									
8									
9									
TOTAL									

BACK NINE

HOLE	PAR	DISTANCE	STROKE INDEX	FAIRWAY	HAZARD	PUTTS	SCORE	+ / -	
10									
11									
12									
13									
14									
15									
16									
17									
18									
TOTAL									

GAME RECAP			
FRONT 9 STROKES		BACK 9 STROKES	
FRONT 9 ADJUSTED SCORE		BACK 9 ADJUSTED SCORE	
TOTAL STROKES		TOTAL ADJUSTED SCORE	

STROKE RECAP			
EAGLES		BIRDIES	
PARS		BOGEYS	
DOUBLE BOGEYS		OTHER	
PENALTY STROKES		PUTTS	
FAIRWAY SHOTS			

NOTES / AREAS FOR IMPROVEMENT

SCORE CARD

LOCATION			COURSE				
PAR		DATE		START TIME		FINISH TIME	
WEATHER & WIND			OTHER PLAYERS				
TEE COLOR			HANDICAP		HOLES PLAYED		

FRONT NINE									
HOLE	PAR	DISTANCE	STROKE INDEX	FAIRWAY	HAZARD	PUTTS	SCORE	+ / -	
1									
2									
3									
4									
5									
6									
7									
8									
9									
TOTAL									

BACK NINE									
HOLE	PAR	DISTANCE	STROKE INDEX	FAIRWAY	HAZARD	PUTTS	SCORE	+ / -	
10									
11									
12									
13									
14									
15									
16									
17									
18									
TOTAL									

GAME RECAP			
FRONT 9 STROKES		BACK 9 STROKES	
FRONT 9 ADJUSTED SCORE		BACK 9 ADJUSTED SCORE	
TOTAL STROKES		TOTAL ADJUSTED SCORE	

STROKE RECAP			
EAGLES		BIRDIES	
PARS		BOGEYS	
DOUBLE BOGEYS		OTHER	
PENALTY STROKES		PUTTS	
FAIRWAY SHOTS			

NOTES / AREAS FOR IMPROVEMENT

SCORE CARD

LOCATION				COURSE				
PAR		DATE		START TIME		FINISH TIME		
WEATHER & WIND				OTHER PLAYERS				
TEE COLOR				HANDICAP		HOLES PLAYED		

FRONT NINE									
HOLE	PAR	DISTANCE	STROKE INDEX	FAIRWAY	HAZARD	PUTTS	SCORE	+ / -	
1									
2									
3									
4									
5									
6									
7									
8									
9									
TOTAL									

BACK NINE									
HOLE	PAR	DISTANCE	STROKE INDEX	FAIRWAY	HAZARD	PUTTS	SCORE	+ / -	
10									
11									
12									
13									
14									
15									
16									
17									
18									
TOTAL									

GAME RECAP			
FRONT 9 STROKES		BACK 9 STROKES	
FRONT 9 ADJUSTED SCORE		BACK 9 ADJUSTED SCORE	
TOTAL STROKES		TOTAL ADJUSTED SCORE	

STROKE RECAP			
EAGLES		BIRDIES	
PARS		BOGEYS	
DOUBLE BOGEYS		OTHER	
PENALTY STROKES		PUTTS	
FAIRWAY SHOTS			

NOTES / AREAS FOR IMPROVEMENT

....

....

....

....

....

....

....

....

....

....

....

....

SCORE CARD

LOCATION		COURSE			
PAR		DATE		START TIME		FINISH TIME	
WEATHER & WIND		OTHER PLAYERS		
TEE COLOR		HANDICAP		HOLES PLAYED	

FRONT NINE

HOLE	PAR	DISTANCE	STROKE INDEX	FAIRWAY	HAZARD	PUTTS	SCORE	+ / -	
1									
2									
3									
4									
5									
6									
7									
8									
9									
TOTAL									

BACK NINE

HOLE	PAR	DISTANCE	STROKE INDEX	FAIRWAY	HAZARD	PUTTS	SCORE	+ / -	
10									
11									
12									
13									
14									
15									
16									
17									
18									
TOTAL									

GAME RECAP			
FRONT 9 STROKES		BACK 9 STROKES	
FRONT 9 ADJUSTED SCORE		BACK 9 ADJUSTED SCORE	
TOTAL STROKES		TOTAL ADJUSTED SCORE	

STROKE RECAP			
EAGLES		BIRDIES	
PARS		BOGEYS	
DOUBLE BOGEYS		OTHER	
PENALTY STROKES		PUTTS	
FAIRWAY SHOTS			

NOTES / AREAS FOR IMPROVEMENT

SCORE CARD

LOCATION		COURSE			
PAR	DATE	START TIME		FINISH TIME	
WEATHER & WIND		OTHER PLAYERS			
TEE COLOR		HANDICAP		HOLES PLAYED	

FRONT NINE									
HOLE	PAR	DISTANCE	STROKE INDEX	FAIRWAY	HAZARD	PUTTS	SCORE	+ / -	
1									
2									
3									
4									
5									
6									
7									
8									
9									
TOTAL									

BACK NINE									
HOLE	PAR	DISTANCE	STROKE INDEX	FAIRWAY	HAZARD	PUTTS	SCORE	+ / -	
10									
11									
12									
13									
14									
15									
16									
17									
18									
TOTAL									

GAME RECAP			
FRONT 9 STROKES		BACK 9 STROKES	
FRONT 9 ADJUSTED SCORE		BACK 9 ADJUSTED SCORE	
TOTAL STROKES		TOTAL ADJUSTED SCORE	

STROKE RECAP			
EAGLES		BIRDIES	
PARS		BOGEYS	
DOUBLE BOGEYS		OTHER	
PENALTY STROKES		PUTTS	
FAIRWAY SHOTS			

NOTES / AREAS FOR IMPROVEMENT

SCORE CARD

LOCATION				COURSE				
PAR		DATE		START TIME		FINISH TIME		
WEATHER & WIND				OTHER PLAYERS				
TEE COLOR				HANDICAP		HOLES PLAYED		

FRONT NINE									
HOLE	PAR	DISTANCE	STROKE INDEX	FAIRWAY	HAZARD	PUTTS	SCORE	+ / -	
1									
2									
3									
4									
5									
6									
7									
8									
9									
TOTAL									

BACK NINE									
HOLE	PAR	DISTANCE	STROKE INDEX	FAIRWAY	HAZARD	PUTTS	SCORE	+ / -	
10									
11									
12									
13									
14									
15									
16									
17									
18									
TOTAL									

GAME RECAP			
FRONT 9 STROKES		BACK 9 STROKES	
FRONT 9 ADJUSTED SCORE		BACK 9 ADJUSTED SCORE	
TOTAL STROKES		TOTAL ADJUSTED SCORE	

STROKE RECAP			
EAGLES		BIRDIES	
PARS		BOGEYS	
DOUBLE BOGEYS		OTHER	
PENALTY STROKES		PUTTS	
FAIRWAY SHOTS			

NOTES / AREAS FOR IMPROVEMENT

....

....

....

....

....

....

....

....

....

....

....

....

SCORE CARD

LOCATION		COURSE			
PAR		DATE		START TIME		FINISH TIME	
WEATHER & WIND		OTHER PLAYERS			
TEE COLOR		HANDICAP		HOLES PLAYED	

FRONT NINE

HOLE	PAR	DISTANCE	STROKE INDEX	FAIRWAY	HAZARD	PUTTS	SCORE	+ / -	
1									
2									
3									
4									
5									
6									
7									
8									
9									
TOTAL									

BACK NINE

HOLE	PAR	DISTANCE	STROKE INDEX	FAIRWAY	HAZARD	PUTTS	SCORE	+ / -	
10									
11									
12									
13									
14									
15									
16									
17									
18									
TOTAL									

GAME RECAP			
FRONT 9 STROKES		BACK 9 STROKES	
FRONT 9 ADJUSTED SCORE		BACK 9 ADJUSTED SCORE	
TOTAL STROKES		TOTAL ADJUSTED SCORE	

STROKE RECAP			
EAGLES		BIRDIES	
PARS		BOGEYS	
DOUBLE BOGEYS		OTHER	
PENALTY STROKES		PUTTS	
FAIRWAY SHOTS			

NOTES / AREAS FOR IMPROVEMENT

· ·

SCORE CARD

LOCATION				COURSE				
PAR		DATE		START TIME		FINISH TIME		
WEATHER & WIND				OTHER PLAYERS				
TEE COLOR				HANDICAP		HOLES PLAYED		

FRONT NINE									
HOLE	PAR	DISTANCE	STROKE INDEX	FAIRWAY	HAZARD	PUTTS	SCORE	+ / -	
1									
2									
3									
4									
5									
6									
7									
8									
9									
TOTAL									

BACK NINE									
HOLE	PAR	DISTANCE	STROKE INDEX	FAIRWAY	HAZARD	PUTTS	SCORE	+ / -	
10									
11									
12									
13									
14									
15									
16									
17									
18									
TOTAL									

GAME RECAP			
FRONT 9 STROKES		BACK 9 STROKES	
FRONT 9 ADJUSTED SCORE		BACK 9 ADJUSTED SCORE	
TOTAL STROKES		TOTAL ADJUSTED SCORE	

STROKE RECAP			
EAGLES		BIRDIES	
PARS		BOGEYS	
DOUBLE BOGEYS		OTHER	
PENALTY STROKES		PUTTS	
FAIRWAY SHOTS			

NOTES / AREAS FOR IMPROVEMENT

SCORE CARD

LOCATION				COURSE			
PAR		DATE		START TIME		FINISH TIME	
WEATHER & WIND				OTHER PLAYERS			
TEE COLOR				HANDICAP		HOLES PLAYED	

FRONT NINE									
HOLE	PAR	DISTANCE	STROKE INDEX	FAIRWAY	HAZARD	PUTTS	SCORE	+ / -	
1									
2									
3									
4									
5									
6									
7									
8									
9									
TOTAL									

BACK NINE									
HOLE	PAR	DISTANCE	STROKE INDEX	FAIRWAY	HAZARD	PUTTS	SCORE	+ / -	
10									
11									
12									
13									
14									
15									
16									
17									
18									
TOTAL									

GAME RECAP			
FRONT 9 STROKES		BACK 9 STROKES	
FRONT 9 ADJUSTED SCORE		BACK 9 ADJUSTED SCORE	
TOTAL STROKES		TOTAL ADJUSTED SCORE	

STROKE RECAP			
EAGLES		BIRDIES	
PARS		BOGEYS	
DOUBLE BOGEYS		OTHER	
PENALTY STROKES		PUTTS	
FAIRWAY SHOTS			

NOTES / AREAS FOR IMPROVEMENT

SCORE CARD

LOCATION				COURSE				
PAR		DATE		START TIME		FINISH TIME		
WEATHER & WIND				OTHER PLAYERS				
TEE COLOR				HANDICAP		HOLES PLAYED		

FRONT NINE									
HOLE	PAR	DISTANCE	STROKE INDEX	FAIRWAY	HAZARD	PUTTS	SCORE	+ / -	
1									
2									
3									
4									
5									
6									
7									
8									
9									
TOTAL									

BACK NINE									
HOLE	PAR	DISTANCE	STROKE INDEX	FAIRWAY	HAZARD	PUTTS	SCORE	+ / -	
10									
11									
12									
13									
14									
15									
16									
17									
18									
TOTAL									

GAME RECAP			
FRONT 9 STROKES		BACK 9 STROKES	
FRONT 9 ADJUSTED SCORE		BACK 9 ADJUSTED SCORE	
TOTAL STROKES		TOTAL ADJUSTED SCORE	

STROKE RECAP			
EAGLES		BIRDIES	
PARS		BOGEYS	
DOUBLE BOGEYS		OTHER	
PENALTY STROKES		PUTTS	
FAIRWAY SHOTS			

NOTES / AREAS FOR IMPROVEMENT

....

....

....

....

....

....

....

....

....

....

....

....

SCORE CARD

LOCATION				COURSE				
PAR		DATE		START TIME		FINISH TIME		
WEATHER & WIND				OTHER PLAYERS				
TEE COLOR				HANDICAP		HOLES PLAYED		

FRONT NINE								
HOLE	PAR	DISTANCE	STROKE INDEX	FAIRWAY	HAZARD	PUTTS	SCORE	+ / -
1								
2								
3								
4								
5								
6								
7								
8								
9								
TOTAL								

BACK NINE								
HOLE	PAR	DISTANCE	STROKE INDEX	FAIRWAY	HAZARD	PUTTS	SCORE	+ / -
10								
11								
12								
13								
14								
15								
16								
17								
18								
TOTAL								

GAME RECAP			
FRONT 9 STROKES		BACK 9 STROKES	
FRONT 9 ADJUSTED SCORE		BACK 9 ADJUSTED SCORE	
TOTAL STROKES		TOTAL ADJUSTED SCORE	

STROKE RECAP			
EAGLES		BIRDIES	
PARS		BOGEYS	
DOUBLE BOGEYS		OTHER	
PENALTY STROKES		PUTTS	
FAIRWAY SHOTS			

NOTES / AREAS FOR IMPROVEMENT

SCORE CARD

LOCATION				COURSE			
PAR		DATE		START TIME		FINISH TIME	
WEATHER & WIND				OTHER PLAYERS			
TEE COLOR				HANDICAP		HOLES PLAYED	

FRONT NINE									
HOLE	PAR	DISTANCE	STROKE INDEX	FAIRWAY	HAZARD	PUTTS	SCORE	+ / -	
1									
2									
3									
4									
5									
6									
7									
8									
9									
TOTAL									

BACK NINE									
HOLE	PAR	DISTANCE	STROKE INDEX	FAIRWAY	HAZARD	PUTTS	SCORE	+ / -	
10									
11									
12									
13									
14									
15									
16									
17									
18									
TOTAL									

GAME RECAP			
FRONT 9 STROKES		BACK 9 STROKES	
FRONT 9 ADJUSTED SCORE		BACK 9 ADJUSTED SCORE	
TOTAL STROKES		TOTAL ADJUSTED SCORE	

STROKE RECAP			
EAGLES		BIRDIES	
PARS		BOGEYS	
DOUBLE BOGEYS		OTHER	
PENALTY STROKES		PUTTS	
FAIRWAY SHOTS			

NOTES / AREAS FOR IMPROVEMENT

SCORE CARD

LOCATION		COURSE		
PAR	DATE	START TIME	FINISH TIME	
WEATHER & WIND		OTHER PLAYERS		
TEE COLOR		HANDICAP	HOLES PLAYED	

FRONT NINE								
HOLE	PAR	DISTANCE	STROKE INDEX	FAIRWAY	HAZARD	PUTTS	SCORE	+ / -
1								
2								
3								
4								
5								
6								
7								
8								
9								
TOTAL								

BACK NINE								
HOLE	PAR	DISTANCE	STROKE INDEX	FAIRWAY	HAZARD	PUTTS	SCORE	+ / -
10								
11								
12								
13								
14								
15								
16								
17								
18								
TOTAL								

GAME RECAP			
FRONT 9 STROKES		BACK 9 STROKES	
FRONT 9 ADJUSTED SCORE		BACK 9 ADJUSTED SCORE	
TOTAL STROKES		TOTAL ADJUSTED SCORE	

STROKE RECAP			
EAGLES		BIRDIES	
PARS		BOGEYS	
DOUBLE BOGEYS		OTHER	
PENALTY STROKES		PUTTS	
FAIRWAY SHOTS			

NOTES / AREAS FOR IMPROVEMENT

....

....

....

....

....

....

....

....

....

....

....

....

SCORE CARD

LOCATION				COURSE				
PAR		DATE		START TIME		FINISH TIME		
WEATHER & WIND				OTHER PLAYERS				
TEE COLOR				HANDICAP		HOLES PLAYED		

FRONT NINE									
HOLE	PAR	DISTANCE	STROKE INDEX	FAIRWAY	HAZARD	PUTTS	SCORE	+ / -	
1									
2									
3									
4									
5									
6									
7									
8									
9									
TOTAL									

BACK NINE									
HOLE	PAR	DISTANCE	STROKE INDEX	FAIRWAY	HAZARD	PUTTS	SCORE	+ / -	
10									
11									
12									
13									
14									
15									
16									
17									
18									
TOTAL									

GAME RECAP			
FRONT 9 STROKES		BACK 9 STROKES	
FRONT 9 ADJUSTED SCORE		BACK 9 ADJUSTED SCORE	
TOTAL STROKES		TOTAL ADJUSTED SCORE	

STROKE RECAP			
EAGLES		BIRDIES	
PARS		BOGEYS	
DOUBLE BOGEYS		OTHER	
PENALTY STROKES		PUTTS	
FAIRWAY SHOTS			

NOTES / AREAS FOR IMPROVEMENT

SCORE CARD

LOCATION				COURSE			
PAR		DATE		START TIME		FINISH TIME	
WEATHER & WIND				OTHER PLAYERS			
TEE COLOR				HANDICAP		HOLES PLAYED	

FRONT NINE									
HOLE	PAR	DISTANCE	STROKE INDEX	FAIRWAY	HAZARD	PUTTS	SCORE	+ / -	
1									
2									
3									
4									
5									
6									
7									
8									
9									
TOTAL									

BACK NINE									
HOLE	PAR	DISTANCE	STROKE INDEX	FAIRWAY	HAZARD	PUTTS	SCORE	+ / -	
10									
11									
12									
13									
14									
15									
16									
17									
18									
TOTAL									

GAME RECAP			
FRONT 9 STROKES		BACK 9 STROKES	
FRONT 9 ADJUSTED SCORE		BACK 9 ADJUSTED SCORE	
TOTAL STROKES		TOTAL ADJUSTED SCORE	

STROKE RECAP			
EAGLES		BIRDIES	
PARS		BOGEYS	
DOUBLE BOGEYS		OTHER	
PENALTY STROKES		PUTTS	
FAIRWAY SHOTS			

NOTES / AREAS FOR IMPROVEMENT

SCORE CARD

LOCATION				COURSE			
PAR		DATE		START TIME		FINISH TIME	
WEATHER & WIND				OTHER PLAYERS			
TEE COLOR				HANDICAP		HOLES PLAYED	

FRONT NINE								
HOLE	PAR	DISTANCE	STROKE INDEX	FAIRWAY	HAZARD	PUTTS	SCORE	+ / -
1								
2								
3								
4								
5								
6								
7								
8								
9								
TOTAL								

BACK NINE								
HOLE	PAR	DISTANCE	STROKE INDEX	FAIRWAY	HAZARD	PUTTS	SCORE	+ / -
10								
11								
12								
13								
14								
15								
16								
17								
18								
TOTAL								

GAME RECAP			
FRONT 9 STROKES		BACK 9 STROKES	
FRONT 9 ADJUSTED SCORE		BACK 9 ADJUSTED SCORE	
TOTAL STROKES		TOTAL ADJUSTED SCORE	

STROKE RECAP			
EAGLES		BIRDIES	
PARS		BOGEYS	
DOUBLE BOGEYS		OTHER	
PENALTY STROKES		PUTTS	
FAIRWAY SHOTS			

NOTES / AREAS FOR IMPROVEMENT

. . . .

. . . .

. . . .

. . . .

. . . .

. . . .

. . . .

. . . .

. . . .

. . . .

. . . .

SCORE CARD

LOCATION		COURSE			
PAR		DATE		START TIME	FINISH TIME
WEATHER & WIND		OTHER PLAYERS			
TEE COLOR		HANDICAP		HOLES PLAYED	

FRONT NINE									
HOLE	PAR	DISTANCE	STROKE INDEX	FAIRWAY	HAZARD	PUTTS	SCORE	+ / -	
1									
2									
3									
4									
5									
6									
7									
8									
9									
TOTAL									

BACK NINE									
HOLE	PAR	DISTANCE	STROKE INDEX	FAIRWAY	HAZARD	PUTTS	SCORE	+ / -	
10									
11									
12									
13									
14									
15									
16									
17									
18									
TOTAL									

GAME RECAP			
FRONT 9 STROKES		BACK 9 STROKES	
FRONT 9 ADJUSTED SCORE		BACK 9 ADJUSTED SCORE	
TOTAL STROKES		TOTAL ADJUSTED SCORE	

STROKE RECAP			
EAGLES		BIRDIES	
PARS		BOGEYS	
DOUBLE BOGEYS		OTHER	
PENALTY STROKES		PUTTS	
FAIRWAY SHOTS			

NOTES / AREAS FOR IMPROVEMENT

SCORE CARD

LOCATION				COURSE				
PAR		DATE		START TIME		FINISH TIME		
WEATHER & WIND				OTHER PLAYERS				
TEE COLOR				HANDICAP		HOLES PLAYED		

FRONT NINE									
HOLE	PAR	DISTANCE	STROKE INDEX	FAIRWAY	HAZARD	PUTTS	SCORE	+ / -	
1									
2									
3									
4									
5									
6									
7									
8									
9									
TOTAL									

BACK NINE									
HOLE	PAR	DISTANCE	STROKE INDEX	FAIRWAY	HAZARD	PUTTS	SCORE	+ / -	
10									
11									
12									
13									
14									
15									
16									
17									
18									
TOTAL									

GAME RECAP			
FRONT 9 STROKES		BACK 9 STROKES	
FRONT 9 ADJUSTED SCORE		BACK 9 ADJUSTED SCORE	
TOTAL STROKES		TOTAL ADJUSTED SCORE	

STROKE RECAP			
EAGLES		BIRDIES	
PARS		BOGEYS	
DOUBLE BOGEYS		OTHER	
PENALTY STROKES		PUTTS	
FAIRWAY SHOTS			

NOTES / AREAS FOR IMPROVEMENT

SCORE CARD

LOCATION				COURSE				
PAR		DATE		START TIME		FINISH TIME		
WEATHER & WIND				OTHER PLAYERS				
TEE COLOR				HANDICAP		HOLES PLAYED		

FRONT NINE									
HOLE	PAR	DISTANCE	STROKE INDEX	FAIRWAY	HAZARD	PUTTS	SCORE	+ / -	
1									
2									
3									
4									
5									
6									
7									
8									
9									
TOTAL									

BACK NINE									
HOLE	PAR	DISTANCE	STROKE INDEX	FAIRWAY	HAZARD	PUTTS	SCORE	+ / -	
10									
11									
12									
13									
14									
15									
16									
17									
18									
TOTAL									

GAME RECAP			
FRONT 9 STROKES		BACK 9 STROKES	
FRONT 9 ADJUSTED SCORE		BACK 9 ADJUSTED SCORE	
TOTAL STROKES		TOTAL ADJUSTED SCORE	

STROKE RECAP			
EAGLES		BIRDIES	
PARS		BOGEYS	
DOUBLE BOGEYS		OTHER	
PENALTY STROKES		PUTTS	
FAIRWAY SHOTS			

NOTES / AREAS FOR IMPROVEMENT

SCORE CARD

LOCATION				COURSE				
PAR		DATE		START TIME		FINISH TIME		
WEATHER & WIND				OTHER PLAYERS				
TEE COLOR				HANDICAP		HOLES PLAYED		

FRONT NINE								
HOLE	PAR	DISTANCE	STROKE INDEX	FAIRWAY	HAZARD	PUTTS	SCORE	+ / -
1								
2								
3								
4								
5								
6								
7								
8								
9								
TOTAL								

BACK NINE								
HOLE	PAR	DISTANCE	STROKE INDEX	FAIRWAY	HAZARD	PUTTS	SCORE	+ / -
10								
11								
12								
13								
14								
15								
16								
17								
18								
TOTAL								

GAME RECAP			
FRONT 9 STROKES		BACK 9 STROKES	
FRONT 9 ADJUSTED SCORE		BACK 9 ADJUSTED SCORE	
TOTAL STROKES		TOTAL ADJUSTED SCORE	

STROKE RECAP			
EAGLES		BIRDIES	
PARS		BOGEYS	
DOUBLE BOGEYS		OTHER	
PENALTY STROKES		PUTTS	
FAIRWAY SHOTS			

NOTES / AREAS FOR IMPROVEMENT

....

....

....

....

....

....

....

....

....

....

....

....

SCORE CARD

LOCATION		COURSE	

PAR		DATE		START TIME		FINISH TIME	

WEATHER & WIND		OTHER PLAYERS	

TEE COLOR		HANDICAP		HOLES PLAYED	

FRONT NINE

HOLE	PAR	DISTANCE	STROKE INDEX	FAIRWAY	HAZARD	PUTTS	SCORE	+ / -	
1									
2									
3									
4									
5									
6									
7									
8									
9									
TOTAL									

BACK NINE

HOLE	PAR	DISTANCE	STROKE INDEX	FAIRWAY	HAZARD	PUTTS	SCORE	+ / -	
10									
11									
12									
13									
14									
15									
16									
17									
18									
TOTAL									

GAME RECAP			
FRONT 9 STROKES		BACK 9 STROKES	
FRONT 9 ADJUSTED SCORE		BACK 9 ADJUSTED SCORE	
TOTAL STROKES		TOTAL ADJUSTED SCORE	

STROKE RECAP			
EAGLES		BIRDIES	
PARS		BOGEYS	
DOUBLE BOGEYS		OTHER	
PENALTY STROKES		PUTTS	
FAIRWAY SHOTS			

NOTES / AREAS FOR IMPROVEMENT

SCORE CARD

LOCATION				COURSE				
PAR		DATE		START TIME		FINISH TIME		
WEATHER & WIND				OTHER PLAYERS				
TEE COLOR				HANDICAP		HOLES PLAYED		

FRONT NINE									
HOLE	PAR	DISTANCE	STROKE INDEX	FAIRWAY	HAZARD	PUTTS	SCORE	+ / -	
1									
2									
3									
4									
5									
6									
7									
8									
9									
TOTAL									

BACK NINE									
HOLE	PAR	DISTANCE	STROKE INDEX	FAIRWAY	HAZARD	PUTTS	SCORE	+ / -	
10									
11									
12									
13									
14									
15									
16									
17									
18									
TOTAL									

GAME RECAP			
FRONT 9 STROKES		BACK 9 STROKES	
FRONT 9 ADJUSTED SCORE		BACK 9 ADJUSTED SCORE	
TOTAL STROKES		TOTAL ADJUSTED SCORE	

STROKE RECAP			
EAGLES		BIRDIES	
PARS		BOGEYS	
DOUBLE BOGEYS		OTHER	
PENALTY STROKES		PUTTS	
FAIRWAY SHOTS			

NOTES / AREAS FOR IMPROVEMENT

....

....

....

....

....

....

....

....

....

....

....

....

SCORE CARD

LOCATION				COURSE				
PAR		DATE		START TIME		FINISH TIME		
WEATHER & WIND				OTHER PLAYERS				
TEE COLOR				HANDICAP		HOLES PLAYED		

FRONT NINE									
HOLE	PAR	DISTANCE	STROKE INDEX	FAIRWAY	HAZARD	PUTTS	SCORE	+ / -	
1									
2									
3									
4									
5									
6									
7									
8									
9									
TOTAL									

BACK NINE									
HOLE	PAR	DISTANCE	STROKE INDEX	FAIRWAY	HAZARD	PUTTS	SCORE	+ / -	
10									
11									
12									
13									
14									
15									
16									
17									
18									
TOTAL									

GAME RECAP			
FRONT 9 STROKES		BACK 9 STROKES	
FRONT 9 ADJUSTED SCORE		BACK 9 ADJUSTED SCORE	
TOTAL STROKES		TOTAL ADJUSTED SCORE	

STROKE RECAP			
EAGLES		BIRDIES	
PARS		BOGEYS	
DOUBLE BOGEYS		OTHER	
PENALTY STROKES		PUTTS	
FAIRWAY SHOTS			

NOTES / AREAS FOR IMPROVEMENT

SCORE CARD

LOCATION				COURSE				
PAR		DATE		START TIME		FINISH TIME		
WEATHER & WIND				OTHER PLAYERS				
TEE COLOR				HANDICAP		HOLES PLAYED		

FRONT NINE									
HOLE	PAR	DISTANCE	STROKE INDEX	FAIRWAY	HAZARD	PUTTS	SCORE	+ / -	
1									
2									
3									
4									
5									
6									
7									
8									
9									
TOTAL									

BACK NINE									
HOLE	PAR	DISTANCE	STROKE INDEX	FAIRWAY	HAZARD	PUTTS	SCORE	+ / -	
10									
11									
12									
13									
14									
15									
16									
17									
18									
TOTAL									

GAME RECAP			
FRONT 9 STROKES		BACK 9 STROKES	
FRONT 9 ADJUSTED SCORE		BACK 9 ADJUSTED SCORE	
TOTAL STROKES		TOTAL ADJUSTED SCORE	

STROKE RECAP			
EAGLES		BIRDIES	
PARS		BOGEYS	
DOUBLE BOGEYS		OTHER	
PENALTY STROKES		PUTTS	
FAIRWAY SHOTS			

NOTES / AREAS FOR IMPROVEMENT

....

....

....

....

....

....

....

....

....

....

....

....

SCORE CARD

LOCATION				COURSE				
PAR		DATE		START TIME		FINISH TIME		
WEATHER & WIND				OTHER PLAYERS				
TEE COLOR				HANDICAP		HOLES PLAYED		

FRONT NINE									
HOLE	PAR	DISTANCE	STROKE INDEX	FAIRWAY	HAZARD	PUTTS	SCORE	+ / -	
1									
2									
3									
4									
5									
6									
7									
8									
9									
TOTAL									

BACK NINE									
HOLE	PAR	DISTANCE	STROKE INDEX	FAIRWAY	HAZARD	PUTTS	SCORE	+ / -	
10									
11									
12									
13									
14									
15									
16									
17									
18									
TOTAL									

GAME RECAP			
FRONT 9 STROKES		BACK 9 STROKES	
FRONT 9 ADJUSTED SCORE		BACK 9 ADJUSTED SCORE	
TOTAL STROKES		TOTAL ADJUSTED SCORE	

STROKE RECAP			
EAGLES		BIRDIES	
PARS		BOGEYS	
DOUBLE BOGEYS		OTHER	
PENALTY STROKES		PUTTS	
FAIRWAY SHOTS			

NOTES / AREAS FOR IMPROVEMENT

....

....

....

....

....

....

....

....

....

....

....

....

SCORE CARD

LOCATION				COURSE				
PAR		DATE		START TIME		FINISH TIME		
WEATHER & WIND				OTHER PLAYERS				
TEE COLOR				HANDICAP		HOLES PLAYED		

FRONT NINE

HOLE	PAR	DISTANCE	STROKE INDEX	FAIRWAY	HAZARD	PUTTS	SCORE	+ / -	
1									
2									
3									
4									
5									
6									
7									
8									
9									
TOTAL									

BACK NINE

HOLE	PAR	DISTANCE	STROKE INDEX	FAIRWAY	HAZARD	PUTTS	SCORE	+ / -	
10									
11									
12									
13									
14									
15									
16									
17									
18									
TOTAL									

GAME RECAP			
FRONT 9 STROKES		BACK 9 STROKES	
FRONT 9 ADJUSTED SCORE		BACK 9 ADJUSTED SCORE	
TOTAL STROKES		TOTAL ADJUSTED SCORE	

STROKE RECAP			
EAGLES		BIRDIES	
PARS		BOGEYS	
DOUBLE BOGEYS		OTHER	
PENALTY STROKES		PUTTS	
FAIRWAY SHOTS			

NOTES / AREAS FOR IMPROVEMENT

....

....

....

....

....

....

....

....

....

....

....

....

SCORE CARD

LOCATION				COURSE				
PAR		DATE		START TIME		FINISH TIME		
WEATHER & WIND				OTHER PLAYERS				
TEE COLOR				HANDICAP		HOLES PLAYED		

FRONT NINE									
HOLE	PAR	DISTANCE	STROKE INDEX	FAIRWAY	HAZARD	PUTTS	SCORE	+ / -	
1									
2									
3									
4									
5									
6									
7									
8									
9									
TOTAL									

BACK NINE									
HOLE	PAR	DISTANCE	STROKE INDEX	FAIRWAY	HAZARD	PUTTS	SCORE	+ / -	
10									
11									
12									
13									
14									
15									
16									
17									
18									
TOTAL									

GAME RECAP			
FRONT 9 STROKES		BACK 9 STROKES	
FRONT 9 ADJUSTED SCORE		BACK 9 ADJUSTED SCORE	
TOTAL STROKES		TOTAL ADJUSTED SCORE	

STROKE RECAP			
EAGLES		BIRDIES	
PARS		BOGEYS	
DOUBLE BOGEYS		OTHER	
PENALTY STROKES		PUTTS	
FAIRWAY SHOTS			

NOTES / AREAS FOR IMPROVEMENT

SCORE CARD

LOCATION				COURSE			
PAR		DATE		START TIME		FINISH TIME	
WEATHER & WIND				OTHER PLAYERS			
TEE COLOR				HANDICAP		HOLES PLAYED	

FRONT NINE

HOLE	PAR	DISTANCE	STROKE INDEX	FAIRWAY	HAZARD	PUTTS	SCORE	+ / -	
1									
2									
3									
4									
5									
6									
7									
8									
9									
TOTAL									

BACK NINE

HOLE	PAR	DISTANCE	STROKE INDEX	FAIRWAY	HAZARD	PUTTS	SCORE	+ / -	
10									
11									
12									
13									
14									
15									
16									
17									
18									
TOTAL									

GAME RECAP			
FRONT 9 STROKES		BACK 9 STROKES	
FRONT 9 ADJUSTED SCORE		BACK 9 ADJUSTED SCORE	
TOTAL STROKES		TOTAL ADJUSTED SCORE	

STROKE RECAP			
EAGLES		BIRDIES	
PARS		BOGEYS	
DOUBLE BOGEYS		OTHER	
PENALTY STROKES		PUTTS	
FAIRWAY SHOTS			

NOTES / AREAS FOR IMPROVEMENT

. . . .

. . . .

. . . .

. . . .

. . . .

. . . .

. . . .

. . . .

. . . .

. . . .

. . . .

SCORE CARD

LOCATION				COURSE			
PAR		DATE		START TIME		FINISH TIME	
WEATHER & WIND				OTHER PLAYERS			
TEE COLOR				HANDICAP		HOLES PLAYED	

FRONT NINE									
HOLE	PAR	DISTANCE	STROKE INDEX	FAIRWAY	HAZARD	PUTTS	SCORE	+ / -	
1									
2									
3									
4									
5									
6									
7									
8									
9									
TOTAL									

BACK NINE									
HOLE	PAR	DISTANCE	STROKE INDEX	FAIRWAY	HAZARD	PUTTS	SCORE	+ / -	
10									
11									
12									
13									
14									
15									
16									
17									
18									
TOTAL									

GAME RECAP			
FRONT 9 STROKES		BACK 9 STROKES	
FRONT 9 ADJUSTED SCORE		BACK 9 ADJUSTED SCORE	
TOTAL STROKES		TOTAL ADJUSTED SCORE	

STROKE RECAP			
EAGLES		BIRDIES	
PARS		BOGEYS	
DOUBLE BOGEYS		OTHER	
PENALTY STROKES		PUTTS	
FAIRWAY SHOTS			

NOTES / AREAS FOR IMPROVEMENT

SCORE CARD

LOCATION				COURSE				
PAR		DATE		START TIME		FINISH TIME		
WEATHER & WIND				OTHER PLAYERS				
TEE COLOR				HANDICAP		HOLES PLAYED		

FRONT NINE									
HOLE	PAR	DISTANCE	STROKE INDEX	FAIRWAY	HAZARD	PUTTS	SCORE	+ / -	
1									
2									
3									
4									
5									
6									
7									
8									
9									
TOTAL									

BACK NINE									
HOLE	PAR	DISTANCE	STROKE INDEX	FAIRWAY	HAZARD	PUTTS	SCORE	+ / -	
10									
11									
12									
13									
14									
15									
16									
17									
18									
TOTAL									

GAME RECAP			
FRONT 9 STROKES		BACK 9 STROKES	
FRONT 9 ADJUSTED SCORE		BACK 9 ADJUSTED SCORE	
TOTAL STROKES		TOTAL ADJUSTED SCORE	

STROKE RECAP			
EAGLES		BIRDIES	
PARS		BOGEYS	
DOUBLE BOGEYS		OTHER	
PENALTY STROKES		PUTTS	
FAIRWAY SHOTS			

NOTES / AREAS FOR IMPROVEMENT

....

....

....

....

....

....

....

....

....

....

....

....

SCORE CARD

LOCATION				COURSE				
PAR		DATE		START TIME		FINISH TIME		
WEATHER & WIND				OTHER PLAYERS				
TEE COLOR				HANDICAP		HOLES PLAYED		

FRONT NINE									
HOLE	PAR	DISTANCE	STROKE INDEX	FAIRWAY	HAZARD	PUTTS	SCORE	+ / -	
1									
2									
3									
4									
5									
6									
7									
8									
9									
TOTAL									

BACK NINE									
HOLE	PAR	DISTANCE	STROKE INDEX	FAIRWAY	HAZARD	PUTTS	SCORE	+ / -	
10									
11									
12									
13									
14									
15									
16									
17									
18									
TOTAL									

GAME RECAP			
FRONT 9 STROKES		BACK 9 STROKES	
FRONT 9 ADJUSTED SCORE		BACK 9 ADJUSTED SCORE	
TOTAL STROKES		TOTAL ADJUSTED SCORE	

STROKE RECAP			
EAGLES		BIRDIES	
PARS		BOGEYS	
DOUBLE BOGEYS		OTHER	
PENALTY STROKES		PUTTS	
FAIRWAY SHOTS			

NOTES / AREAS FOR IMPROVEMENT

....

....

....

....

....

....

....

....

....

....

....

....

SCORE CARD

LOCATION				COURSE			
PAR		DATE		START TIME		FINISH TIME	
WEATHER & WIND				OTHER PLAYERS			
TEE COLOR				HANDICAP		HOLES PLAYED	

FRONT NINE

HOLE	PAR	DISTANCE	STROKE INDEX	FAIRWAY	HAZARD	PUTTS	SCORE	+ / -	
1									
2									
3									
4									
5									
6									
7									
8									
9									
TOTAL									

BACK NINE

HOLE	PAR	DISTANCE	STROKE INDEX	FAIRWAY	HAZARD	PUTTS	SCORE	+ / -	
10									
11									
12									
13									
14									
15									
16									
17									
18									
TOTAL									

GAME RECAP			
FRONT 9 STROKES		BACK 9 STROKES	
FRONT 9 ADJUSTED SCORE		BACK 9 ADJUSTED SCORE	
TOTAL STROKES		TOTAL ADJUSTED SCORE	

STROKE RECAP			
EAGLES		BIRDIES	
PARS		BOGEYS	
DOUBLE BOGEYS		OTHER	
PENALTY STROKES		PUTTS	
FAIRWAY SHOTS			

NOTES / AREAS FOR IMPROVEMENT

....

....

....

....

....

....

....

....

....

....

....

....

SCORE CARD

LOCATION				COURSE				
PAR		DATE		START TIME		FINISH TIME		
WEATHER & WIND				OTHER PLAYERS				
TEE COLOR				HANDICAP		HOLES PLAYED		

FRONT NINE									
HOLE	PAR	DISTANCE	STROKE INDEX	FAIRWAY	HAZARD	PUTTS	SCORE	+ / -	
1									
2									
3									
4									
5									
6									
7									
8									
9									
TOTAL									

BACK NINE									
HOLE	PAR	DISTANCE	STROKE INDEX	FAIRWAY	HAZARD	PUTTS	SCORE	+ / -	
10									
11									
12									
13									
14									
15									
16									
17									
18									
TOTAL									

GAME RECAP			
FRONT 9 STROKES		BACK 9 STROKES	
FRONT 9 ADJUSTED SCORE		BACK 9 ADJUSTED SCORE	
TOTAL STROKES		TOTAL ADJUSTED SCORE	

STROKE RECAP			
EAGLES		BIRDIES	
PARS		BOGEYS	
DOUBLE BOGEYS		OTHER	
PENALTY STROKES		PUTTS	
FAIRWAY SHOTS			

NOTES / AREAS FOR IMPROVEMENT

....

....

....

....

....

....

....

....

....

....

....

....

NOTES

SCORE RECAP

DATE	COURSE	FRONT 9	BACK 9	TOTAL

DATE	COURSE	FRONT 9	BACK 9	TOTAL

Thankyou for your purchase!

If you get the chance, we would love an honest review
on the location in which you purchased this book. We
are a small business that appreciates every review!

Printed in Great Britain
by Amazon